ABOUT THE AUTHOR

Qudsia Akhtar is a Manchester-based poet who is currently undertaking a PhD at the University of Salford. Her work has appeared in *Acumen, The Tower Poetry Anthology, The Ofi Press,* and *Poetry Birmingham Literary Journal.*

www.couldseeher.co.uk
insta: @couldseeher

Qudsia Akhtar
Khamoshi

VERVE
POETRY PRESS
BIRMINGHAM

PUBLISHED BY VERVE POETRY PRESS
https://vervepoetrypress.com
mail@vervepoetrypress.com

FIRST PUBLISHED MAR 2022

Printed and bound in the UK
by ImprintDigital, Exeter

ISBN: 978-1-913917-06-7

Cover art by Marya Akhtar

CONTENTS

Khamoshi

Part One

The eye of existence is not familiar with me,
I rise trembling, afraid to show myself.

Muhammad Iqbal, *Secrets of the Self.*

I

One's life
can experience
many worlds,

step
into the psyche
and then out

into the day.
Harsh lighting
awakens senses,

unfolds
dreams
and tries them

on. We slip
into states,
just like

in dreams, bird
turns to bomb.
     Silence

narrates our fears,
sleep stained
by the dark

under our masks.
Paper dreams
tear with

the slightest shift
of mind, far
from complete.

Dreams swell
with feeling, suit
our inner lives.

Fighting with
Friction, voices
duel.

How many
selves can
one host share?

I shuffle
characters
like a deck.

I s-s-s-spark
the wire,
drive the car.

How many roles
can one
jar hold?

When I feel
my heartbeat
alone, I hear

my voice call
my self
imposter

and the self
collapses
in silence.

K

H

A

M

O

S

H

I

II

I was cast out of my motherland
by the hands of my ancestors.
I see flashes of salted black plums,
spitting sugarcanes, chai in bowls,
jinn stories in the dark, and hear home
in the pronunciation of my name.
It still lingers like the scent of smoke

from the hookah pipe. I was eleven
when I first found that fear suited
my face and that in the noir-nights
I resembled the black of a crow,
I pecked her soil, tasted its fruit,
and then fell asleep on her manjee.

The dark
witnessed
the start
of my fall.

Dark drowned the light. Warm tiles
burnt my feet, the ant colony built
trails in uncooked rice, and those girls
starry-eyed, auctioned to entitled men,
paid with the currency of their lives.

Who am I
to speak?
Coaxed
to suspect.

"You desire to feed on men,
to destroy our heritage!"
This is what they say.

So, I let go. Shed my skin. Kissed my hands
goodbye and felt the blood race
in the hands that replaced My own.
My own.
My own.

III

Summer. I am twenty-two.
We take photographs
searching for sunspots.
To comfort our conflicted bodies,
in my bedroom, I read to you
my thoughts, poem and journal.
I look up to see her face and smile,
she saw the serious emptiness.

She saw my skin, a sheath searching
for the sword of home, of hope.
The blade bearing the debt of history
and aching for a fleshed-out place,
a marked space made for me, I lost,
I lost when I left the land that held
my breath. I try, oh, I try to transcend
my body.

My hands, my feet, my actions,
they speak, utter words a clipped
tongue cannot reach. I spend my
mornings in retreat, on last night's
reflections, hoping that I wake
in a different body.

IV

You can find me under a tall tree
seeking to embody a hair of grass,
a potted plant, a bewitching bird.
Can I be from here if my roots
lie elsewhere? Like tangled wire,
my fingers fumble to find the source.
I am the rose, I am the exiled heart.

I trace wire to socket, loosen
my grip on my hyphenated existence.
I am what I am not, a British-whatnot,
a coloured nervous condition
destined to pick my self apart.
My Baba Aadam dealt with his two-part
persona, good and bad. It shadows
my ego, reflects my fruitless fall.

I long to see motherland, caress
the flesh of her hills even though I
was cast out from heaven a long time ago.
Now faith is in faces of flowers,
a Rose Mallow belongs here, there,
everywhere. I stand outside myself,

my home, my language, my rights.
Unlike the foreign wind that blows
life into the rose, I bring death
to all my experiences, for my colour
is a border. I am a distortion of lenses.
The ego is like a mirror, and mine
reflects the times, a judgement day
complete with signs.

I guard the other,
I hold the honour,
I grasp hope to let go
of who I once
never was.

My mother-tongue
isolates me,
tosses me away.

Caught
between cultures which both
shun me.

I am a liability. Listen,
do these hands not feel like yours?
Can one experience diaspora
in the body?

The questions
eat me.

I sit to write at my desk, I see
glass door, a growing garden,
cat on brick wall. I fear this, them.
I cannot welcome the unknown.
The cat destroys the plants, the cat
carries the same desire as I,
it yearns to feed, I turn back to write.

I must unearth my ego, my fragile wires
like a mismatched map claim to see
the substance of me. I piece together
a past of violence and the path to carve
gifted to me by my dead forefathers
and mothers.

I
lead
crusades
against
myself.

I embody The Partition, split since birth.
Tell me your stories they say.
Teach me your ways.
I watch *my people* build brick-houses
and lock me out for I am not their past,
not ripe, not desi enough.

Just a shade close.

V

the eleventh of march of the years before '96
i was elsewhere   descending from some place
to another space
when was the first time you ever felt your eyes open?

STOP

to consider the sky above you   so vast   so blue
and you tell yourself whoever made that made you
and then you smile because you're so caught up
in racial identity that you grab the shovel
dig a hole and bury Iqbal's books hoping that a flower
will shoot from the ground bearing leaves of hopeful words
that tell you soon we shall belong somewhere.

VI

This feeling of isolation stays
like a stone in my holey shoe.

Part Two

Their sea is silent, like dew,
But my dew is storm-ridden, like the ocean.

Muhammad Iqbal, *Secrets of the Self.*

In the Mouth of Tradition

1

She is falling into the pit –
the mouth of tradition

where sleeping girls wait,
past and present,

their bodies fertile, ripe,
ready to be touched,

to be swallowed whole.
Marriage stitches the mouth,

sealing the curse of femininity.
The curse. The curse. The curse.

2

Cycling through the heat of June,
she passed black bins, crushed
Rubicon cans, and an empty
field.

School is hung
in the wardrobe
with her uniform.

This was the last light
of summer she would keep.

3

A sleeping body woke
with a startling scream:

*"He says, he says, he says,
I must, I must, I must."*

And then she sees
a circle of roses, girls

sitting cross-legged,
muttering words of a prayer:

*"First came the gifts from paradise,
a man who lusts for wild eyes,*

*brown pools of honey, we can't fight
his biology. And then came the promises*

*of keeping his name and his body,
whilst he burns you with fiery eyes.*

*Then came the shattered shame,
shards of honour, with only you to blame."*

4

The arrival of gifts was strange.
Gold bangles, a red lehenga,
promises of a brighter sun
with him rather than childhood
and choice.

She had 'the talk' with her parents,
the dealers of her fate, coaxing
her into the pit.

He will command
the sun to rise,
the grass to grow,
the meeting of sea and sand
is all in his hands.

And she found
that those lyrics of songs,
those romanced passages
in books,
no longer
applied
to her.

5

"We worship the ways of man,
his caramel words, his sticky eyes

that fix to our bodies keeping
us women together in praise

of his offerings of love. Why,
in brief moments we feel loved."

The girl lowered her palms
and slipped off tradition's tongue

into
the abyss.

6

Her parents made her bed
and now she must lie in it.

7

The faces of girls, muddy and morose
stare at her. They were buried.

This is a pit, a darkness, their femininity
a fertiliser to bear fruit for his soil.

Girls, wilted flowers for him
to crush into the page, edible

or poisonous. Girls, bound in extremes,
the wrath of the female is to be cursed

in this pitiful pit of tradition with snapped
stems, buried innocence, sucked on, chewed

and then swallowed, swamped in their sweaty
flesh. Sweaty flesh is what it feels like,

what it feels like to be a woman,
to be seen and not heard.

On Both Sides

You can't be in two places at once.
Can't tear a limb to bridge the gap
of two languages.

A cellular displacement causes
abnormalities. A two-headed
creature considered a monstrosity

is a simple genetic malfunction.
This is rooted in science,
not just society.

The Year of the Girl

Riot.
I first disobeyed my mother by being born.
They called it the Year of the Girl.

A plague.
An eclipse.
Pits of apples
held nests of worms.
I ate from plates,
drank out of clay cups
that were never mine.
My mother, like her mother,
carried the burden of womanhood
as she sang tradition's song,
his divine ways, his glory, his sage.
We are poisonous. We provoke his rage.

Riot.
I was a child
when I first felt the riot in me
as I saw other girls
become bone and teeth.
Their tongues dry
like July's heat
thirsty for life
that offers shade.

Riot.
And the father I loved,
the brother I raised,
and the mother who muttered
plans to plot my death.
When they took my voice,
the finger still pointed at me.

Riot.

Slow Burn

It was an ordinary day. The sky was plain,
the morning stained with the Sunday feeling,

nothing to do, nowhere to be. Until
the buffalo did not wake, died in her sleep.

A woman pelts the pomegranate
with the back of her spoon

and the ruby arils become loose and fall,
scatter like teeth into the bowl. She crushes

the foetus-sized black peppercorns, pickles
the chillies and mangoes, preserves them in a jar

and glances over at the buffalo deep in sleep
with no offerings of milk or motherhood.

Her garden surviving, patches of growth.
The mint leaves grow next to a single

flower carefully positioned in the ground.
Whispers of wind spread the smell of mint

distracting the eye from the uneven land
and conceal the warmth of a resting

newborn, asleep in the soil's womb,
smothered with hands, tears, and kisses.

Residue

I woke up to traces of you
in the silvery sky framed
by the window as daylight
spilt into my room.

I can taste traces of you
on my tongue, in my language
as I speak your syllables
to fill the black hole in me.

Does the sky talk of humans?
Does the sky share our sorrows?

I write you into words,
lick the envelope, drop you
in the post, sending you miles
away, only to wake up
with you again.

Inheritance

My cupped hands carry ancient
lines of dark rooms dense with
hookah, chai, and mad men who
bang on the daff and chant:

"Oraat mard ko dosak mei lakae jai gee".

My cupped hands are fed, wed to
speculative phrases, bound in his
interpretations, fluent with
accusations. I am made of his rib
yet I deserve his spit. Ancient lines
of moonlit nights, prayers, and men
who gather to recite:

"Oraat mard ko dosak mei lakae jai gee".

My cupped hands bear the burden of
hell, him, and hope. For my hands hold
the creation of sin. So, he points his finger
to the thick text of rulings, circling vague
phrases and says:

"recite: Oraat mard ko dosak mei lakae jai gee."
        A woman will take a man to hell.

Erased

She is a cautionary tale of the feminine curse,
people read her like braille and spit out the words
and fill in the blanks with her name, alongside countless
women who made the same mistake. They quote God

and mourn, for a female's rash choice is her own, and
a mother should feel the emptiness in her womb because
she raised a sin. Her name rests on tongues that only know her
cursed infamy. Her name rests on her mother's shelf like a trophy
    of shame.

But, I remember the day your bedroom door would not open
and your mum came to find us trapped, crying on the floor.

Fourteen

Music class. Headphones on. Blocking
the bickering classmates out, listening
to Taylor Swift yearn for her long-distance
lover and how he had told her
her blue eyes had shone like stars and stuff.

Later that day, my friends and I
stood in the middle of the field.
This redheaded boy walked over
and told us how our complexions
looked dirty. A dirty brown and stuff.

I Hear Noor Jamal Singing

I hear Noor Jamal singing,
my fathers, brothers, mothers, sisters sing
the hang-dog, human-song. I hear

the pista-like reeds whip the ground,
labouring lyrical seeds that feed the land
in my sacred mother's hennaed hands.

I hear one father's foot on a tractor,
dogs barking, my children's laughter, and when
God calls, he stops and listens to his Master.

I hear revving rickshaws, bellowing
bulls, bewitching birdsong, bleating
goat, ping-pong gossip,
and my grandfather cycling home
with grapes
    for me to eat
        as the song
            hums on...

Woman, Woman, Woman

The clouds are still
as in a stop-motion frame.
Four birds find
a bony branch to rest
their tired wings.

To our ears,
the travellers of the sky
merely chirp and screech
stirring the day to life.
But some birds hear and chatter.

For below them,
in a sugarcane field lies
a body parched by the sun,
the tongue a hardened
shell, shoeless and limp.

The soulless soil defiled
by sin, the cane stalks
seem to have shape-shifted
into snakes,
and that body

displayed to all
like some relic,
testimony to her impurity,
broken, bruised,
deformed.

That body
carries a shame that
will not be spoken of
by fearful people
who christen her:

"Woman, Woman, Woman!"

And the birds,
they chatter
and move on to
some other perch,
some other story.

My Dad is a Terrorist

My dad has a grey beard, pumps the car's
stereo with a man reciting Allah's words,
carries Surah Yaseen in his car's glove
compartment, eats with his right hand,
greets his neighbours, visits the mosque,
cares for the elderly, gives to charity,
prays five times a day and eats his fruit,
loves my mum's curry, has jokes up his
sleeves. He wears my mum's
prescribed glasses to read the Quran but
after he reads Surah Fatiha, he falls asleep.

Yes, that's my dad –
        the terrorist.

A Mother's Landay

I always wake counting my children
even the ones who only exist in memories.

Face Painting

My sister sealed your mouth
with a slab of black paint.
Your body is ghosting the mask.
A grim ghoul, glimpses
of The Exorcist, the other-
worldly demon possesses you.

As I ran, I noticed keen
kittens alert to our presence
in wait for mother-cat,
you shouted scaring them.
And then, they had gone.

Summer's heat penetrated
our feet as we ran, first,
second, third floor reaching
the sky of the village –
a balcony with its view

of the native river trying
to resurface the loss of home,
once transparent, now muddy
like the paint on your face
mixed with sweat from the chase.

I told you to sit whilst
your mouth melted like ice
cream dripping off its cone.

A Brief Encounter

You stood afar on a sunny day,
the black veil across your face
concealing the eternal flame
of faith.

All around me, faces shoot
past, left and right, but you
stand in the shade and visions
of a past I've painted with words

come to life.

Your choice
of black, a statement,
a life enslaved to devotion.
You and me as little as tasbih
beads, searching for meaning.

You have a dream,
I have a dream to wake up
to some truth
to the prayers we read, to urge
our tongue to translate meaning.

You have a dream,
I have a dream to touch
the naked flame.

Post 9/11

Post 9/11 –
   the song of myself died

Hijabs became a global threat
banned burkas
banned burkinis
because no woman chooses to cover
said a man somewhere in France

On a London tube
   a girl walking home
her hijab is ripped off by a stranger
   poor guy
he was only doing her a favour

Meditation

The other night, I felt your presence.
So, I left my door half open
to let you enter my chamber
and comfort my seeking soul.

For you, I have dainty wings.
I am a moth tapping window-
glass begging
to be let into your light.

You are the cascading water
dripping from the fountainhead,
as clear and as reflective,
you are how I perceive you.

I see a morsel of you
in every beautiful being –
a fan-shaped gingko leaf –
a surma-lined tiger's eye.

Punish a Muslim Day

Every terror attack,
every tragedy on the front page
reminds me of the time I sat
in my high school English class
and the teacher would write *terrorist*
on the whiteboard and turn and say:
What does that word make you think of?
And I would hold

my breath.

The Mothers of All Believers

Let me tell you a tale of the women in me.
Women who sit under the shade of that tree
and listen to the rush of the river, feel the
plush-like texture of a fresh date plucked
and heaped in palms of children who chase
one another after the communal prayer.

Let me tell you a tale of the women in me.
Women who wrap themselves in sheets of
faith in hope to hold a divine message,
to nurture the seeds of a child and plant a tree
that bows to Him.

These women fought endless wars in backdrops
of sacred deserts, in the confines of their home,
in the hearts of others, and still, they stand against
the heat even if it burns their backs.

Let me tell you a tale of the women in me,
they do not need your approval to feel complete.

A Seeker's Ghazal

Let me sew smooth webs for you always,
to trap your love, suck your blood, always.

Stoned from floating fantasies, I drink
from your boundless fruitful flood, always.

Let me beat the daff, feel the echo
of the eastern mountains thud, always.

For your hope holds the sun's intensity,
nurtures my small divine bud, always.

I dance naked in fiery deserts
to the holy song you hummed always

of starless nights, drunken daffs, and my
Qudsia's lust for the blest flood, always.

Shikwa

Shut the day out and absorb the music.
Women crushing chillies in their fist
fuelling the fire.   I said listen
as they lead the bulls across to plough
the paddy field –

my grandma is one of the women.

Shut the day out and absorb the music.
Flustered red-hot children cry as the women walk,
baskets balanced on the head,
full of chapattis to feed
the men –

my grandma is one of the women.

Shut the day out and absorb the music
of the colourless compromise,
where the women are told men
only fertilise the soil
     and   them.

Shut the day out and absorb their stare.
The eyes sing shattered songs
that lose their range when far from home.

My grandma is one of the women.

Part Three

Tongue-tied, thou art in pain:
Cast thyself upon the fire, like rue!
Like the bell, break silence at last, and
from every limb
utter forth a lamentation!

Muhammad Iqbal, *Secrets of the Self.*

VII

In me there is a migration song replaying its refrain of sorrow,
for a signature split the land searing the tongues of many.

A migration song of swarming massacres, camps, genocides,
of colonial and ethnic legacies, a parting of body and mind.

Bloodshed bodies borders, borders bodies bloodshed.
A man wakes his wife, weds gold to her wrist and runs

hiding in a field. Homeless. Hopeless. Uncertain
of the future, a raw grainy undeveloped film.

Lahore train station, crowded and confused,
multitudes lost in search of an idea, of home.

Parents unable to fend, to feed. They feel
the thumping hearts of their children,

this great migration, a clouded sun
it takes and takes and takes every light

that speaks human, speaks life.
Their innocence left in the old world,

the life before in distant dreams,
the life before the bloody streams.

VIII

Dil Dil Pakistan...

Yes, I'd like a cake with the
Green and White flag, please.

IX

It's Black Day today. I protested in my sleep.
Kashmir burns before my eyes, children hung on trees,
hear the rhythm of their death tolls rise   black
black

Life is not symmetrical. I pray
for children living under
dark archways, bloodbaths,
all the under shadows of us and them.
I long for narratives that gift peace,
not a marketing strategy, I pray.

We are politicised, our bodies policed
and then I realise
my breath is bait to increase hate.
These words are a personal confession
of me.

Why can someone else seal my fate?
Identities are born from rage, snapped
into place by people claiming a face.
You are Pakistani. You are Indian. You are Kashmiri. You are British.
You are what you are. At the edge,
drawing close to the silence,
non-linear lines of thought tracing
their way through history, to the making,
to the making of me.

I do not preach, I pray, I pray, I pray
and then I turn to witness violated flesh
        when I hear the cries
of children whose tongues are drawn out
and cut.

Blood turns
black on
this blackest
black
day.

Black, my
Uniform for
the protest
song.

Black invades my dreams. I feel the darkest screams.
Every child I see sparks sadness in me, for I think
of their hollow breaths beating   black
black

X

I am three years old. Head down,
follow my feet, mum's hand leads
me to the hairdressers. Sit down.
Stare at my lap. Listen to them talk,
I don't understand the words.
I understand a feeling. Glance up to see
Al Jinnah's photograph; framed
on the wall. I knew he was important.
I knew he demanded my respect.
I concluded –

    all good men look like Al-Jinnah.

XI

we inhabit systems   i'm a shape-shifter   i warp into expectations

once i spent so long trying to decode

what was in my mother's head that i forgot to step out of it

can remember the exact time i first realised i felt trapped

you misplace an object   search

for days to find it   weeks later   it shows up in the most obvious place

this is how this works

i am five years old   i take off my sandals   i smell heat

i remember a hue   mess around with the   RGB

tool on photoshop to create a taupe filter that's the shade

of the water   i step in   my feet can't touch the floor   i hold on

to the edge   my skirt spreads like octopus legs   water reaches

my ears   i don't feel afraid   i don't feel anything   i feel in between

something   water feels like heavy air   it weighs you down

until my cousin pulls me out   she's used to danger   this is her home

and i sit on the floor   somewhere away

from home and wonder what i just felt

even the water told me i didn't belong

and then i remembered who i was.

XII

I am in between something.
What lies ahead is pixelated,
my past echoes in archways.

I carry
myself
into
the night.

XIII

Every year,
I decide
renovation

is key for
belonging,
what survives

are cracked clay
masks, homeless
characters.

I discard
empty traits
I used to

shield constant
states of fear
for a future

far away.
Clung onto
daggers of

feelings, felt
frustrated
when I lost

the right to
my skin, I,
a loaned word

mispronounced,
entertain
the strangers

in my house,
I draw back
the curtains

hoping light
will burn
them out.

XIV

What does the British-Pakistani want?
Our bruised bodies birth broken ideas,
language jarred, fixed to bump the head
of the hyphens. Us, limited beings fluent
in tongues of passivity, speak syllables
that serve the hands of our masters
who have guided us to our realities.

We are more than a body.
We are an Historical Myth.
Mistranslated, dislocated, eliminated.
We emerge from the paddy fields,
from fingers delving in sacred soils,
from the lullabies of the working day.
Our feet have walked this land,
held the hand of elders as they speak
of history, of a time where we loved endlessly.
Now they are their accent.

We are praised when we hate ourselves,
a modern-day public flogging. Our rallies cry:

We are not like *them,*

Their ways: medieval,

Their dreams: inhuman,

Their hopes: oppressive.

For those in the back,
we are not like *them.*

XV

My Nana Abu taught my mum
how to serve English Tea correctly,
how to perfect her manners
to the English
standard.

XVI

Tears tattooed
onto my face.
I promote

the sadness
of the
human race.

Stained
by shadows
of beginnings,

of seeds
never sowed
on dry land.

To like me,
I must be
approved,

stamped by
white hands,
filtered by

tick boxes,
glad to be
saved from

my face.
You want to
read me

when I bleed
to be like
you. You. You.

You want to
read me
when I need

to accept
your forced
gift. Gift. Gift.

I am what
I cannot
be.

XVII

In my mind's eye, I see the dead,
I think of them now. I think of now.
Like a foreign tongue, I hear their tone.
I think of how, I think of how,
out of fear, they fed on flesh
to escape certain death. Their bodies
beating in the heat hiding from
the ones preparing the feast.

In my mind's eye, I hold their breath.
I think of now. I think of now.
The mouth of bigotry lusts for blood.
I think of how, I think of how,
its claws sinking in soil, its ancient
mind focused on flesh, always hungry
for its land. The beast stands, teeth
deep into skins that have been shed,
waiting for us.

We stay here. Palms on grass, head
toward heaven, up there, flock of birds.
Tell me what you feel, not what you are.
Tell you what I feel, not what I will never be.
Lend me your heart and I will wear it.
Lend me your voice and I will sing it.

Love is like an orange tree, soaking in sunlight.
Roots firm in soil, poised perfectly. Watch
how the tree gives to palms, never stops
bearing fruit for the human, always feeds
because that is what it means to love.

Part Four

I am a wave and I will come to rest in
his sea,
That I may make the glistening pearl
mine own.
I who am drunken with the wine of his
song
draw life from the breath of his words.

Muhammad Iqbal, *Secrets of the Self.*

XVIII

Nothing is ever complete. A poem
ripens with age. Never ready to eat.
They demand silence, silence, silence
to transport you to an ink-splattered
galaxy where visionaries greet you.

No art is a complete thought. We live
in possibilities, introductions, endless
speeches of renewal. Libraries carry
the voices of words, of ideas that tease
revolutionary realities.

What am I? Oh! Where am I?
These feet have felt
chains of difference
claim ownership
of my body.

I embody protest. A one-woman show
until I meet the rest. I wear the flag
of hope, of resistance to the cruel
narratives of the past, the present,
and the future. I embody stories
of silent fields, hennaed hands,
mystical nights filled with stars,
ghouls in graveyards, and homes
burning with the fire for food.
I encompass all truths that wait
in all things¹; sea, bird, tree.

I envision these feet in frames
to furnish the rooms filled
with audiences. Only creation
offers me wings to soar lands
where sleepless souls dance
to the flute singing songs
of liberation. Art, my dear,
demands the presence
of the artist.

XIX

New Orleans issues an apology,
eleven Italians killed. France,
Strasbourg's synagogue kicked
off the plinth, rise in anti-Semitic
attacks, and bodies drop
in Christchurch, New Zealand,
Charleston Church, Manchester
Arena, the church in Rouen,
and the fifteen-year-old black boy
stands in Texas shouting

Don't shoot, I'm human.

Don't shoot. I'm human.

XX

What is the price of this body?
Hands grip the lathi, rioting
for breath, for freedom. Bodies
butchered, thrown in villages,
railway attacks, dog stands
in tracks waiting for its scraps.
Camps swarming with parched
tongues. Quaid-i-Azam
imprinted in our minds,
his khadi sherwani,
his existence the fourteenth
of August.

Lend your ear
to these sounds of the past,
to the lives lost in the chaos
of collective identity. I salute
the painful positions of 'I',
whipping hearts foraging
for the fight for home.
A home is the prize.
The pain is the price.

XXI

I am not
a single
entity.

I unlock
pasts with the
key of longing

to create
narratives
to carve

complete stories.
Can Herstory
be rewritten?

Our violent
past projects
into aggression.

I pay
homage
to all

the voices
in me.

We are victims.
We are not victims.

XXII

I cannot write. I cannot write of who I am,
afraid of sentimentalism. Poetry,
a gift I stumbled upon, a privilege
to speak society. Iqbal envisioned
Motherland and I still yearn for it.

I see a craft to create a cycle of thought,
using condensed images to riot for us.
Voiceless, we buy into moulded liberty.
Sleep with money, wake, trapped
in the same loveless cycle.

I am more than my body.
I am more than this shell.

I do not only address today. I sing riots
for tomorrow. I interrupt the song
of change and sing my verse. I exist
to exist for us. Project our voice
to say:

I carry the charge of a thousand feet.
They thrash against the barriers
of history and wake the dead
to riot, to riot with me.

XXIII

I've existed
in many
states,

been used
by people who
see their needs.

I fit shoes
Of -isms,
people spit

racism,
sexism,
radicalism,

as if I
own the
words.

I will tell
my people,
I will tell you

when you tell
yours.
Day and night,

I am
the walking
dead.

I linger
in lonely
states until

pages burn
from my
flame.

The page
carries
us.

I take charge,
tell you
I feel.

Histories
of torture,
teach me

I am not
alone, poets
paint periods

with words.
I crave to
speak to souls

not faces.
I pray
my words

are enough.
I can't move
mountains

but I can
move you,
listener,

to give me
my voice
back.

ACKNOWLEDGEMENTS

Thank you Allah for granting me the strength and direction to express myself creatively.

This book is dedicated to my family and friends, my dearest grandparents and parents who sacrificed their dreams for me to live mine, and to all those whom I have met in passing that have shaped and influenced my poetical direction in some way whether consciously or subconsciously.

To Peter Wells and Scott Thurston who have endlessly worked with me to teach me the world of poetry developing my creative practice, and for believing in my visions before their conception.

To the tutors at the University of Salford who have shaped my view of writing and literature tremendously.

I am incredibly indebted to the following journals/schemes for showcasing my work: Tower Poetry, Acumen, The Ofi Press, Poetry Birmingham Literary Journal, and the New Creatives.

And finally, I am incredibly grateful to Stuart at Verve Poetry Press for gifting me this wonderful opportunity and for bringing my work to light!

I have used quotes from Muhammad Iqbal's poetry/philosophy book *Secrets of the Self* (1972).

ABOUT VERVE POETRY PRESS

Verve Poetry Press is a quite new and already prize-winning press that focused initially on meeting a local need in Birmingham - a need for the vibrant poetry scene here in Brum to find a way to present itself to the poetry world via publication. Co-founded by Stuart Bartholomew and Amerah Saleh, it now publishes poets from all corners of the UK - poets that speak to the city's varied and energetic qualities and will contribute to its many poetic stories.

Added to this is a colourful pamphlet series, many featuring poets who have performed at our sister festival - and a poetry show series which captures the magic of longer poetry performance pieces by festival alumni such as Polarbear, Matt Abbott and Imogen Stirling.

The press has been voted Most Innovative Publisher at the Saboteur Awards, and has won the Publisher's Award for Poetry Pamphlets at the Michael Marks Awards.

Like the festival, we strive to think about poetry in inclusive ways and embrace the multiplicity of approaches towards this glorious art.

www.vervepoetrypress.com
@VervePoetryPres
mail@vervepoetrypress.com

Can one experience diaspora / in the body?" Qudsia Akhtar's poems are silted with female loss, a kind of silence that builds slowly inside generations of migrant women. Through partition, nationalism, racism, sex and filial duty, these poems ask to whom do we belong if not our selves? A motherland calls to its daughters; an adopted country demands to hear her voice. Akhtar's language is rich and exact, fearing sentiment, turning on its heel towards a path entirely of its own.'
- Sandeep Parmar

'Qudsia Akhtar's thrilling debut collection Khamoshi (Silence) traces the complexity of living as a British-Pakistani writer with great courage, integrity and insight. Akhtar's vision takes in the broader historical perspectives of the trauma of partition and the experiences of racism and sexism while focusing on the embodied tensions of a self that is never fully at ease with itself: 'I hear / my voice call / my self / imposter.' In dialogue with Muhammed Iqbal's philosophical poem 'The Secrets of the Self', Akhtar asks unflinchingly 'can I be from here if my roots / lie elsewhere?', 'what does the British-Pakistani want?'' can Herstory / be rewritten?', creating a precisely articulated poetry full of vivid images and passionate thinking. If Akhtar does not shy away from the challenges she presents ('the chaos of collective identity'), nevertheless this is an enormously optimistic book in which she wears 'the flag / of hope' whilst paying homage to 'all / the voices / in me.' This is an adept and provocative work which firmly establishes Akhtar as an important new voice for her generation.'
- Scott Thurston

Khamoshi is Qudsia Akhtar's debut full collection.

ISBN 9781913917067

9 781913 917067

UK £9.99 RRP

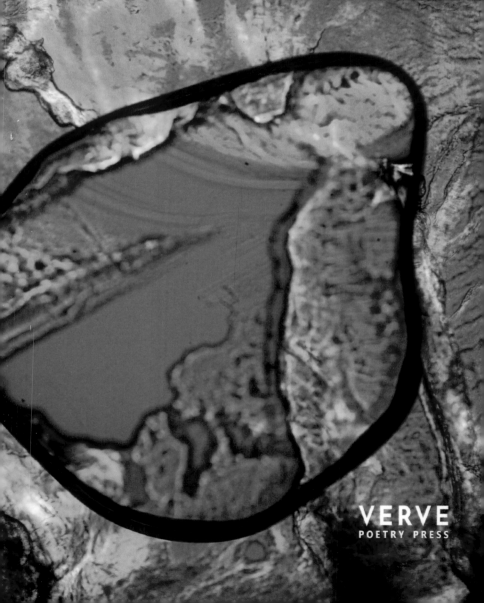

Thin Slices

Caitlin Stobie

VERVE
POETRY PRESS